At the

Who said "he
The sea lion   8
Baby elephant   14
The little goats   20

Who said "hello"?

"This is the zoo, Ben," said Ajay.
"You will like it here."

"HELLO! HELLO!"

Ben said, "Stop, Ajay.
Who said hello?
Who said hello to me?"

"Mum, who said hello to me?"

"Can't you guess?" said Mum.

"Can't you guess who said hello?"

"I can guess," said Liz.
"A parrot."

"Come here, Ben," said Ajay.
"Come and look at this parrot.
It can say hello."

"A parrot can say hello!" said Ben.
"Say hello, parrot. Say hello to me."

The sea lion

"Look at the sea lion," said Liz.

"Yes, Liz," said Mum. "Come and see what it can do."

"Can I get Ben and Ajay?" said Liz.

Mum said, "No.
They want to look at the parrot."

Ajay said, "Look, Ben, here's Kamla."

"Hello, Ben," said Kamla.
"Do you want to see the sea lion?"

"No! I like the parrot.
It can say hello."

"The sea lion can swim," said Kamla.
"And it can play with a ball.
Come and see it, Ben."

"Here's the sea lion, Ben," said Kamla.
"It can play with a ball."

"It can! It's funny," said Ben.
"Come here, Dad, come and look.
This sea lion can play with a ball."

Dad said, "Sea lions like to
play with a ball."

"I like the sea lion," said Ben.
"It can play with a ball.
But it can't say hello.

Come and see the parrot, Dad.
I want the parrot
to say hello to you."

Baby elephant

Ben's dad said,
"Come and look at the baby elephant."

"I can't see the elephant," said Ben.

"Will you help me up?"

"Yes. Can you see now?" said Dad.

"Yes, I can see the elephant in the water," said Ben.

"A baby elephant likes to play in the water," said Dad. "Look at it now!"

Ben said, "Will the mother elephant feed it?"

"No," said Dad. "The zoo man will feed it."

"Here he is," said Ben.

"Here, little elephant," said the zoo man.
"You will like this."

The little goats

"I want to see the goats," said Liz.

"Here they are, Liz."

Ajay said, "We can play with the goats. Here they come."

"That is the mother goat," said Liz, "and her baby is with her."

"The baby goat is funny," said Kamla.
"He can't run fast.
He's too little."

Liz said, "Look at this goat. He wants something."

"Hello, little goat," said Ben. "What do you want?"

"Can't you see?" said Kamla. "He wants to play."

"No," said Ajay.

"He wants something to eat."

"But we can't feed the animals," said Liz.

"The zoo man will feed the goats."